CRIME AND DETECTION

PROTECTING YOURSELF AGAINST CRIMINALS

Crime and Detection series

CRIME AND DETECTION

PROTECTING YOURSELF AGAINST CRIMINALS

JOAN LOCK

MASON CREST PUBLISHERS
www.masoncrest.com

Mason Crest Publishers Inc.
370 Reed Road
Broomall, PA 19008
(866) MCP-BOOK (toll free)
www.masoncrest.com

First printing

1 2 3 4 5 6 7 8 9 10

Library of Congress Cataloging-in-Publication Data on file at the
Library of Congress

ISBN 1-59084-385-1

Editorial and design by
Amber Books Ltd.
Bradley's Close
74–77 White Lion Street
London N1 9PF
www.amberbooks.co.uk

Project Editor: Michael Spilling
Design: Floyd Sayers
Picture Research: Natasha Jones

Printed and bound in Malaysia

Picture credits
Corbis: 6, 11, 16, 18, 22, 25, 26, 29, 33, 35, 38, 40, 44, 45, 49, 52, 54, 59, 65, 74,
76, 80; The Picture Desk, Kobal Collection: 69; PA Photos: 62, 82; Popperfoto: 30,
67, 70, 73, 85, 88; Topham Picturepoint: 8, 10, 12, 13, 15, 19, 20, 23, 42, 46, 47,
50, 56, 57, 61, 66, 79, 83, 86.
Front cover: Corbis (main), Topham Picturepoint (center right and bottom).

CONTENTS

Introduction

From the moment in the Book of Genesis when Cain's envy of his brother Abel erupted into violence, crime has been an inescapable feature of human life. Every society ever known has had its own sense of how things ought to be, its deeply held views on how men and women should behave. Yet in every age there have been individuals ready to break these rules for their own advantage: they must be resisted if the community is to thrive.

This exciting and vividly illustrated new series sets out the history of crime and detection from the earliest times to the present day, from the empires of the ancient world to the towns and cities of the 21st century. From the commandments of the great religions to the theories of modern psychologists, it considers changing attitudes toward offenders and their actions. Contemporary crime is examined in its many different forms: everything from racial hatred to industrial espionage, from serial murder to drug trafficking, from international terrorism to domestic violence.

The series looks, too, at the work of those men and women entrusted with the task of overseeing and maintaining the law, from judges and court officials to police officers and other law enforcement agents. The tools and techniques at their disposal are described and vividly illustrated, and the ethical issues they face concisely and clearly explained.

All in all, the *Crime and Detection* series provides a comprehensive and accessible account of crime and detection, in theory and in practice, past and present.

CHARLIE FULLER

Executive Director, International Association of Undercover Officers

Left: In the United States, reported crime against people in their own homes has steadily fallen over the last 10 years. Studies show that burglars are overwhelmingly male and the majority are aged between 14 and 29 years old.

Personal Property

It is possible to protect yourself and your property without becoming fearful and paranoid. Simply teach yourself to be observant of your surroundings and the people in them and adopt sensible security habits. Prevention is the key. However, should the worst occur, most security experts agree that it is normally safer not to resist violent theft. Your personal safety is more important than your property. This chapter offers a set of simple rules and suggestions to help you protect your property and yourself.

BEFORE YOU LEAVE HOME

- Mark your property.
- Leave any money that you will not need while you are out safely locked up at home.
- Pull your sleeves down to cover any expensive wristwatches, and wear a scarf over gold necklaces, or even consider whether it is worth the risk of wearing them at all.

AWAY FROM HOME

- If you carry a purse, do not let it swing loose on your arm. The safest way to carry it is to put the strap over your head to rest on your shoulder with the strap across your chest and the purse held securely under the opposite arm.
- **Pickpockets** prefer people who carry their wallets in their back pockets ("the sucker pocket," as they call it) or in their breast pockets. Keep your wallet in your front pants pocket.

Left: Passengers at a Metro stop in Washington, D.C. The hustle and bustle of such places, and the fact that people are distracted, makes them popular with pickpockets.

Shoulder bags are favorite targets. Here, the bag is a Karrysafe Screamer, one of a street-safe collection. When a thief pulls hard, the strap detaches and triggers an alarm.

• Do not advertise the whereabouts of your property and money. By taking it out of your pocket or purse more than necessary, you are making it easier for a thief. And do not pat your pocket to make sure your wallet is still there; that just alerts the would-be thief as to what pocket it is in.

• Try to avoid high-crime areas when you are alone.

When you are away from home, watch out for distraction ploys. For example, someone may bump into you "accidentally" and pat you down to see if you are all right. In reality, he or she may be checking to see what possessions you have on you and where. Or, someone may distract you by telling you that you have dropped something. Some thieves will stage a fight or heated argument nearby to attract people's attention while their pickpocket colleagues get to work. Another tactic is to have a person pretend to faint at your feet.

Be extra alert when getting on and off trains, buses, and subways; waiting in line at the grocery store; or when sightseeing in a place you are not familiar with. You will be distracted by the enticing new scenery and will probably be carrying more money than usual. Thieves know this.

AT AUTOMATIC TELLER MACHINES (ATMs)

- Be alert and aware of who is around so that you will not be taken by surprise if you are attacked.
- Do not allow anyone to look over your shoulder while conducting your transaction. By doing so, someone can follow your transaction and learn your PIN number, which gives him or her access to your account.
- If someone tells you that you have dropped some money, retrieve your card before checking whether or not this is true. It is a common

When your attention is elsewhere, you become an easier target for thieves. Backpacks are particularly vulnerable: even if locked, they may be cut open. Make sure you carry money and valuables elsewhere.

distraction scam that gives thieves sufficient time to steal your card when it is ejected from the machine.

CELL PHONES

Use cell phones discreetly, particularly in isolated or high-crime areas. Not only are they likely targets for thieves, but they also distract you when your attention should be centered on your safety and your belongings. In addition, guard your cell phone PIN number as closely as you do that of your credit card.

ON VACATION

Do not put your address on your suitcase because this advertises that your home is empty. Do not pack valuables in the suitcase you intend to check

The endless line for an ATM (Automatic Teller Machine) at the Woodstock 99 Three-Day Festival in Rome, New York. Pickpockets often operate in such busy areas.

At ATMs, make sure that no one is standing right behind you where they can see your PIN number as you type it in. Also, watch out for distraction ploys—someone may try to grab either your cash or your card.

in. Jewelry and other small valuables should remain with you at all times and be carried on board with you in your carry-on baggage. Be vigilant at railroad stations, airports, and in hotel lobbies. Successful thieves dress to look like respectable travelers and hotel guests.

Beware of cute and friendly children who follow you around—they may be planning to steal your valuables. In certain countries, you may find the plight of street children heart-rending. If so, you will benefit them most by donating to a legitimate charity that helps them, not by making yourself vulnerable to having your valuables stolen by them.

CREDIT CARDS

If you have a credit card with a personal identification number (PIN), you must protect it so no one else can get access to your account and go on a spending spree.

• Do not make your PIN number something obvious, like your birth date or social security number.

• Do not write it down anywhere.

• Sign your credit card as soon as you receive it. Destroy the old credit card by cutting across the magnetic strip.

• Be wary of seemingly official phone calls checking on your card's details.

• Make telephone credit card purchases only on a fixed landline, not on a cell phone.

• Do not let your credit card out of your sight in restaurants or retailers. Its magnetic strip can be copied for cloning in seconds, and since you are away from home, it may be a long time before you are aware of what is happening.

• Do not leave valuables in the trunk of the car or even "out of sight" at isolated areas of outstanding beauty, like national monuments.

• Be aware that thieves may be watching out for tourists with rental cars.

• Use a hidden money belt. The visible type, also called a fanny pack, is an easy target for muggers with sharp knives.

• If you must use a backpack, do not put your money in it. Carry your money on the front of your body. Thieves can rob you in a flash when your pack is on your back.

• Keep expensive cameras concealed, if possible. You could carry it in a plastic shopping bag.

• Be wary of people offering to take your camera from you in order to "take your picture with your friend." Many offers are genuine; some are not.

• Use travelers' checks when abroad.

AT THE HOTEL

When booking a hotel room, it is worth asking about the location of the room. Ground-floor rooms and those adjacent to the fire escape are most vulnerable because they are easy to approach and escape from.

• Leave a light and a radio or television on, even when you are out.

• Anyone traveling alone should consider asking at the reception desk for an escort to their rooms and should check the room carefully before the escort leaves.

Cell phones not only attract thieves, who can easily snatch them and run, they may also distract users, making them less aware of approaching danger.

Not all fellow travelers are what they seem. Some are thieves who hang around hotels, railroad stations, and airports waiting for an opportunity to steal luggage from careless passengers.

- Use the hotel safe for valuables.
- Use peepholes and security chains on doors, but do not rely on the chains for total security. It may not be strong enough to resist forced entry.
- Do not open the door (even with the chain on) to an unexpected caller, even if he or she claims to be maintenance staff or room service. Check with reception first.

HOTEL ROOM INVASION

The following true story is a real-life example of what can happen if you are not on the alert in a hotel room. In May 1997, writers Mark Billingham and Peter Cocks were staying at a hotel in Manchester, England, while working on a television series. They decided to have a lazy night, enjoying beer and pizza in front of the TV. Later, Mark answered a knock on their hotel room door, thinking it was a member of the staff who had come to take away their tray.

Instead, three masked men stood there. Mark was instantly smashed in the face and driven back into the room to shouts of, "Down on the floor or you're dead!" The TV sound was turned up to drown out the shouts, and the room was sprayed with the contents of an opened beer bottle. The object was to frighten and confuse.

"They got what they wanted," Mark admits. "In less than a minute, I was bound and gagged face-down on the carpet."

Credit cards were extracted from their wallets and lined up on the carpet in front of them. One of the men knelt down and whispered, "Do what we want or we'll hurt you." Mark was punched in the face to reinforce the message, and Peter had his neck stepped on and what felt like a gun pressed to the back of his neck.

Once PIN numbers were given and watches and cell phones grabbed, the pair hoped it would all be over. But two of the thieves stayed with them while the third went out with the cash cards.

For Mark and Peter, the wait was interminable and terrifying. They had no idea how this was going to end, and any sound they made was greeted with punches or death threats.

In the end, the invaders left the room silently without telling Mark or Peter, who were slow to realize that they were now safe. None of the three men was ever caught, and they left a lasting (and unwelcome) legacy. Mark, who now writes crime fiction, found that the fear felt by the victim has come to influence much of his work.

DANGEROUS COUNTRIES

When visiting most destinations, the personal security precautions mentioned previously are similar to those at home. If you are in any doubt, however, consult government agencies or Web sites for warnings about particular countries. Sometimes, you will be advised simply not to go there at present, and it is as well to follow the advice. Governments may also warn of places where mugging has currently reached **epidemic** proportions.

Do not pay attention if someone says, "Oh, I've been there and had no problem." He or she could just have been lucky. Arm yourself with information so you are not taken unaware.

There is usually some country that travelers are advised not to visit. This may be due to a crime epidemic or social unrest leading to risk of kidnapping for ransom. In some countries, kidnapping for ransom is a common way for criminal gangs to raise funds.

CAMPUS CRIME

Engineering student Ashish Modi became aware that two young men were following him as he headed home to his apartment in Troy, New York. They jumped him, one yelling, "Money! Money!" as he opened a switchblade. Modi told them he was a student and did not have

any money. They knocked him to the ground, crushed his glasses, and shouted that he better have some next time they saw him or else.

Eighteen minutes later, Amit Kekare, another student, was on his back with a knife to his throat and his money being stolen. Of the estimated 10 mugging victims in that spree of November 1 and 2, 2001, five were students at the Rensselaer Polytechnic Institute, and all of them were from overseas.

A public-safety spokesman pointed out that since September 11, 2001, the school had expanded its escort service to serve off-campus residents. Even after hours, if an escort was needed, students were told to contact them.

Victims are not always students. In March 2001, administrator Michael Jackson was mugged in one of the campus restrooms at Columbia in Chicago. His assailant pressed his fingers against Jackson's back to simulate a gun.

Predators and Stalkers

Predators are almost usually male, but not always. Do not automatically trust someone just because she is a woman. Occasionally, a predator works with a woman, using her to help lure victims. It is extremely rare, but a woman can become a solitary predator. However, it is not necessary to live your life in constant fear of predators. You can adopt a few habits, some as simple as walking with confidence, to help prevent you from becoming a victim. Never accept a ride from a stranger. And do not ever go anywhere with someone you do not know. Habits like this will make you feel sure of yourself, and if you look confident, you are less likely to be attacked.

AWAY FROM HOME

Let someone know where you are going. You might find it annoying to have to tell a parent or someone where you are going, but this can become a matter of life or death. While you are out, always carry the phone numbers of family members or a reputable taxi firm to use in an emergency.

Be aware of your surroundings, particularly if you are in a strange area. Think about how you present yourself. For example, walk confidently. A timid and nervous stance can encourage an attack. Try to look as if you know where you are going, even if you do not. Seeming lost may encourage an attacker or give a predator an opportunity to offer assistance. Do not cut yourself off from your surroundings by wearing a hood or using a Walkman or cell phone (unless to call for assistance). The hood will restrict your vision and the earphones your hearing. Your full attention ought to be on your surroundings and the people in them.

Left: German doctor Klaus Wagner became famous as an obsessive stalker of Diana, Princess of Wales, and gained some notoriety in the British press for doing so.

Regular joggers should vary their routes and times to prevent a predator from planning an attack. They should never wear a Walkman. They need all their senses to keep them safe.

Walk along the middle of the sidewalk, and try not to let anyone come up close behind you. If necessary, cross to the other side of the street. Walk toward oncoming traffic so drivers can see you and you avoid the risk of a car pulling up behind you. If you jog regularly, do not let a potential predator predict your route. Be sure to vary it from day to day. Have your house keys ready for use. Fumbling for them at the doorway can offer an opportunity for attack.

PASSWORD TECHNIQUE

If you are responsible for picking up a younger brother or sister from school, work out a password together. Do not choose anything too obvious that others might easily guess. Then, if you are ever unable to meet your brother or sister after school and want to send someone in your place, your brother or sister knows that you have sent this person and it is safe to walk home with them. If you have a parent or babysitter that normally picks you up from school, it is a good idea to have a password with them as well. That way, if someone ever approaches you and says he or she has been sent by your parent, for example, but does not know the password, you know there is something wrong and should get help. Do not reveal the password to anyone, not even your best friend. People talk, and it could become common knowledge and therefore useless. It is a good idea to change the password regularly.

Carry a **personal alarm** and keep it handy. The noise can frighten off an attacker, alert other people, and give you time to escape. But it is no use if you have to search around in your purse or pockets to find it in a crisis.

Learn some simple self-defense techniques and practice them regularly. Most of us are reluctant to hurt others, and women and girls often find it even more difficult to strike out because they have usually had little experience of physical-contact sports or rough-and-tumble play. Consequently, if attacked, they tend to freeze.

At the same time, we should all be aware of how easily we might appear to be a threat to someone alone. You should not walk too near someone else in isolated places or sit too close in an otherwise empty bus or subway. Remember that you, too, can appear threatening.

SELF-DEFENSE

Females in the movies stand there and let themselves be attacked, but that is not a safe, realistic solution. Enroll in proper self-defense classes and practice the moves regularly. You can do this with a brother or sister, a friend, or your parents. However, never let your new expertise make you overconfident. Stay aware and try not to let yourself get into situations in which you are left vulnerable to attack.

Even a physically small and weak person can gain time to escape by striking hard in vulnerable places, such as a man's groin or shins. If attacked, react immediately. The face and head also have several sensitive places. The pain caused by grabbing handfuls of hair and pulling hard while poking your attacker hard in the eyes or hooking your fingers into his nose can disable him long enough for you to escape.

Have a convenient weapon at hand. An umbrella, keys, hair or perfume spray, a rolled-up magazine or newspaper, or a purse can all be used as weapons to help you gain time to escape. Should you be attacked, hit hard, then run fast. Keep in mind, however, that if you do not do these things right the first time, you are in trouble, because it will only anger the

Kickboxing is an excellent form of self-defense. Get fit and learn a few simple self-defense techniques. Practice them regularly, but do not depend entirely on them. Sensible habits are your best defense.

You are much less likely to be attacked if you take a few simple precautions. However, if you are attacked, try to react instantly. Hit and run—fast.

individual, and the anger will be taken out on you. Attempting this may be your only hope, so be forceful when you do.

IF YOU ARE FEELING THREATENED...

• Head for somewhere there are other people, like a gas station, shopping mall, or restaurant.

- Knock on the door of a home with a light on and explain your situation.
- Never be tempted to take a shortcut down an empty lane or alley.

If attacked:

- Shout, scream, and make a lot of noise. This may frighten off your attacker, giving you time to escape.
- Tell onlookers what is happening. They sometimes assume people are just fooling around or think they are witnessing a couple having an argument.
- Onlookers may be reluctant to intervene for fear of looking foolish or having the pair turn on them. Shout, "I am being attacked! Help me! Call the police!"
- Another good way of drawing attention to your situation, particularly if you are attacked indoors, is to shout "Fire!" rather than "Help!" Self-preservation can cause those nearby to find out where these shouts are coming from and why.

IN FAMILIAR PLACES

Watch out for adults who hang around playgrounds or youth clubs for no good reason. Inform someone in charge if you notice any. You can protect yourself by discouraging overly familiar behavior from an adult, even if he or she is someone you should be able to trust, like a youth leader or teacher. Do not be afraid of politely, but firmly, saying "No" to an adult.

CLUBS OR PARTIES

When you are out at clubs or partying with friends, there are a few basic rules to keep in mind. Do not leave your drink unattended. Never accept a drink from a stranger; it could be **spiked**. Never accept a ride home from a stranger. Phone your parents and ask them to pick you up, or carry the phone numbers of a few reliable cab firms and call a taxi. Do not leave alone. Predators watch out for young people leaving clubs and parties alone. Show up with a friend and leave with a friend. Do not be tempted to stay because you are having a good time. Never, ever walk home alone.

TRAVELING SAFELY

By car:

- Some people have a tendency to get into their cars after shopping, eating, or working and then just sit (doing their checkbook or making a list). This leaves them in a highly vulnerable position because a predator will be watching, and this is the perfect opportunity for him to get in the passenger side, put a gun to the driver's head, and tell him or her where to go. As soon as you get into your car, lock the doors and leave.
- Keep your car well-maintained or if you use your parents' car, make sure they do. A breakdown on a lonely road is the last thing you want.
- Carry a cell phone.
- Join an auto club, like AAA.
- Check the back seat before getting in.
- Have your keys ready to open the door, and get in quickly.
- Lock the doors as soon as you get in, and lock the doors as soon as you get out.
- Be vigilant when in parking lots, which are often deserted and badly lit. Try to use one with an attendant.
- If you are bumped by another vehicle on a lonely road, do not get out to discuss the matter there. Indicate that you will drive on and go to a garage or police station.

On public transportation:

- Alone on a bus or subway with someone who makes you feel nervous? Sit near the door or by the **communication alarm** or by the driver.
- Keep valuables nearby; do not place them on the rack overhead or in the aisle.
- Make sure you have any useful weapons (keys, umbrella, etc.) at hand.
- At the next stop, move to a seat where there are more people. If anyone approaches you threateningly, press the communication alarm or alert the driver.

Keeping a car well-maintained helps prevent breakdowns in lonely spots, which may leave the driver (and her family) vulnerable to attack. It is usually best to stay inside your locked car until help arrives. Carrying a cell phone on long car journeys is a useful precaution.

Railroad and bus stations and the paths leading to them can be dangerous places, particularly at night if unmanned and little used. Predators are aware that you have to follow a defined and possibly lonely route to get there and, once there, may have to wait alone. Exercise particular care when entering the station restrooms, which may also be deserted. They isolate you in a confined space and give a predator the opportunity to hide behind a partition or in a vacant toilet, then confront you as you leave your cubicle.

Celebrities and other famous people, like John Lennon, a former member of the '60s band The Beatles, can attract lethal stranger stalkers, but many victims are ordinary people stalked by those with whom they have had a relationship. Here, Lennon is signing an autograph for Mark Chapman, the man who was later to kill him.

STALKERS

It was the stalking of celebrities, including Jodie Foster, Madonna, and, fatally, John Lennon, that brought the problem into the spotlight. But most stalking victims are private citizens. Most, but not all, stalkers are male. Most, but not all, victims are women. Usually, a stalker is someone who once had a relationship with the victim. These are also the stalkers most likely to become violent. Stalkers who are not ex-partners may be friends or acquaintances or even complete strangers. Most stalkers (and their victims) tend to be in their thirties, but they have been known as young as nine years old and as old as 77. The offense is increasing among teenagers. There are many motives for stalking. As well as obsessive "love," it can be revenge that drives them or jealousy of your perceived "advantages." It may even be some imagined insult by you that triggers the situation.

One of the oddest stalking cases took place in Britain. A man had his phone **tapped** while he was temporarily a murder suspect. Eventually, he was released without being charged. However, he turned on the policeman who had listened in to his calls and bombarded him and his family with silent calls and death threats.

Stalking is against the law. California was the first state to legislate against it, and most other states followed suit with versions of their own laws. The Protection from Harassment Act was passed in Britain in 1997. However, just because it is against the law does not mean that a potential stalker will necessarily be deterred. So what can you do to prevent this happening to you and, if it should arise, to stop it?

HOW TO AVOID ACQUIRING A STALKER

Even the most unlikely people can be potential stalkers, while some may be more prone to stalking than others. Be careful, for example, when dealing with someone who is socially incompetent, very shy, and obviously considers him- or herself unattractive to the opposite sex. Always be polite and kind to these people, but bear in mind that if they are unused to such attention, they may read more into your good manners and kindness than you intend. They may think you care deeply about them and become fixated on you. You should also be careful not to give away your personal details, particularly on the Internet.

EAGER BOYFRIEND OR POTENTIAL STALKER?

When you are young, it can be difficult to tell the difference between an eager boyfriend or girlfriend and a potential stalker, but if you think someone is becoming obsessed with you:

• Do not respond to his or her attentions, no matter how flattered you feel. Do not feel guilty about ignoring him or her.

• Make it very clear you are not interested, but do not humiliate the person.

If you suspect you have a stalker:

• Make it very clear that you are not interested.

• Keep records of his or her approaches.

• Save any letters, packages, or e-mails.

• Keep recordings of telephone messages.

• Do not respond to any of this person's letters, phone calls, or e-mails.

• Alter your daily routine and keep it flexible so that a potential stalker cannot get an idea of your movements and start following you.

• Never agree to meet the person.

• Inform friends, neighbors, and family of the situation. They will be able to look out for you, will not be tricked into revealing your details or whereabouts, and could also act as independent witnesses, if necessary.

• If the stalker still persists, inform persons in authority, such as your teacher, your family, and the police.

• Protect yourself by taking the advice in the sections about predators and home security.

• Learn self-defense.

• Screen your calls. If a stalker has your home phone number, consider

Never accompany a stranger to his car, nor let anyone
remain with you while you open yours. Once you are inside
with him, you become very vulnerable.

having an answering machine pick up your calls or get caller ID. Then get an unlisted number. Give out this number only to friends and family, and ask them to keep it secret. Never pick up the phone when the stalker rings. Eventually, he or she may get bored always talking to your answering machine and give up.

- Join an anti-stalking support group.
- Always have a cell phone with you. Remember to keep the batteries charged.
- Consider getting a dog.

FIGHTING BACK

Some female victims in the U.S. have put their experience as stalking victims to good use. Renee Goodale, who was harassed by her **estranged** boyfriend, realized that most people fail to comprehend the violent nature of stalking and founded S.O.S. (Survivors of Stalking). This is a nonprofit organization run by volunteers, with the motto, "Ending the silence that kills." S.O.S. runs community education programs and anti-stalking workshops, produces personal safety publications, and runs a Web site.

Another victim, Dr. Doreen Orion, a psychiatrist stalked by a patient, wrote a book on the subject, *I Know You Really Love Me.* It describes her own case history and others, including David Letterman, Madonna, a woman rabbi, an Olympic athlete, and many others. Dr. Orion also discusses ways to improve anti-stalking laws and gives a guide to organizations that assist victims. She uses the proceeds from her book to maintain an anti-stalking Web site.

CASE HISTORY: THE SMART PREDATOR

Ted Bundy is an infamous example of a murderous predator, and he serves as a useful reminder of two important lessons about predators. The first lesson is that there is no typical "look" to predators. Ted Bundy was absolutely nothing like the stereotypical image of the unattractive loner serial killer who can get a woman only by abducting her. Ted Bundy was a young, handsome, well-dressed, intelligent, and charming law student with a degree in psychology. He abducted, raped, and murdered between 20 and 40 young women in Seattle, Salt Lake City, Colorado, and Florida during the years from 1974 to 1978. His youngest victim was only 12 years old.

Most of the girls were abducted in his car, and to make sure they got into it, he used clever ploys to enlist their sympathy. At university campuses, he would wear his arm in a sling or walk with the aid of crutches. Then he would ask the targeted young woman to give him a hand with his briefcase, packages, or books. This guise (along with his acceptable appearance and

Serial killer Ted Bundy with lawyers in a courtroom. Charged with killing two teenage girls, he had a charming manner and pleasant looks that helped him fool his victims into believing he did not present a threat.

BOTH ENDS OF THE AGE SPECTRUM

We all get crushes when we are young. A nine-year-old boy in Hastings, Michigan, had such a crush, and he broke the anti-stalking law when he called the object of his obsession over 200 times in a few months.

At 77 years of age, James Monk became Britain's oldest convicted stalker in October 1997, when he pleaded guilty to harassing his ex-girlfriend, 55-year-old Mary Sands. He had learned that she was seeing another man (aged 74), so he began plaguing the couple with abusive telephone calls. He also sent her friends explicit photographs and letters about his own relationship with Mary and painted the walls of her house with ugly graffiti.

demeanor) made him seem harmless. On another occasion, he approached a girl in a shopping mall, claiming to be a police officer and telling her that her car had been broken into. He asked her to come and check the damage and contents. She found none, so he said he would take her to the police station where the suspect was being held.

En route, her suspicions grew, particularly when he began going in the wrong direction. She made a grab for the door handle and threw the door open, but Bundy snapped handcuffs on her wrist and pointed a gun at her head. Desperate, she took a chance, opened the door again, and threw herself out onto the road.

Bundy followed her, armed with an iron bar, but lights from an oncoming car illuminated the scene and he fled. Which leads to the second lesson: many others approached by Bundy also survived, either because they refused to go with him or ran away after becoming suspicious once they reached his car.

The moral is: Never, never, never accompany a stranger to his or your car, no matter how harmless and acceptable he or she seems, nor how safe the parking lot appears to be. It takes only a second for someone to strike you and push you into the car or draw a gun. (Vans are even more dangerous than cars. Their bulk can block the view of what is happening, particularly if they are parked alongside a wall.)

CASE HISTORY: DON'T ALWAYS TRUST A WOMAN

In October 1995, in Winchester, England, Rose West was convicted of 10 murders, which she had carried out with her husband, Fred West. He had committed others on his own, but he was able to escape justice by committing suicide in his prison cell. Rose was sentenced to life imprisonment without parole.

FEMALE STALKERS

When Warwick University lecturer Dr. Robert Fine drew back his curtains on a Sunday morning, a woman's face would confront him. When he went for his early morning swim, she would be there, swimming alongside him, staring at him. She was one of his older students who, in 1993, had decided that he had made a pass at her and that, in class, he made it clear to everyone that he lusted after her. She began to follow him ceaselessly.

Banning by the university and a civil action failed to stop her, even after Richard had been awarded £5,000 ($7,500) in damages for harassment and she had been ordered not to go within 200 yards of his home. It was only when he married a fellow lecturer and moved away that the stalking finally ceased. The following year, 1997, the anti-stalking law was passed in Britain to help the growing number of victims obtain protection.

Several of the Wests' victims were young women hitchhikers or others who had been offered a ride when waiting for a bus or walking home. The presence in the car of a motherly looking woman in her thirties doubtless reassured them that they were in no danger. But Rose West was to assist in their torture, rape, and murder.

The appearance of Charlene Williams was equally disarming: the 22-year-old was tiny, slight, and waif-like. In September 1978, she approached 16-year-old Kippi Vaught and 17-year-old Rhonda Scheffler in a Sacramento shopping mall. She suggested that they might like to come to her van and smoke some marijuana. Lying in wait was her boyfriend, Gerald Gallego. The two girls were driven to a deserted spot where, with the assistance of Charlene, they were raped and horribly murdered.

The pair's next victims were younger (14 and 15 years old) and

Gerald Gallego is captured after Mississippi's greatest manhunt. He raped and murdered 10 young women after his girlfriend, Charlene Williams, had helped to entrap them.

SHEILA BELLUSH

Sheila Bellush was sure that Allen Blackthorne, her ex-husband and stalker, would get her in the end, even though she and her family had moved from Texas to Florida in the middle of the night to evade him.

She asked her sister to swear to fulfill two promises should anything happen to her. One was to ensure there was an investigation and the other was to have the well-known, true-crime writer Ann Rule publish her story.

Sadly, something did happen to her. In November 1997, after 10 years of fear, she was brutally murdered in front of her two-year-old quadruplets. The children were spattered with her blood and left alone with her body for many hours.

An investigation eventually revealed that Blackthorne had paid Joey del Toro, a Mexican drug addict, to kill his ex-wife. On July 6, 2000, in Florida, del Toro pleaded guilty to first-degree murder. A little later that day in Texas, Blackthorne, who denied the charge, was also found guilty. Both were sent to jail for life. Ann Rule wrote Sheila's story in *Every Breath You Take*, published in 2001.

were picked up at a county fair in Reno, Nevada. This time, Charlene used the **ruse** of asking them if they would like to make a few dollars delivering pamphlets.

In all, Charlene and Gerald murdered 10 people (including one man). There have been several such serial-killing couples. So, while it is true that women are much less likely to be predators and murderers (only around two percent of serial killers are female), you should always bear in mind that female strangers might also be dangerous.

Home Security

Every member of the family should take an interest in home security. After all, your precious possessions are at risk, as well as your lives. Some of the best aids to home security are the simplest. If you become aware of your surroundings, you will notice when there are strangers around, and making friends with your neighbors means that they will be more likely to watch out for you and notice if any unusual activity is taking place around your home. Remember: burglars like things easy. If your home looks tough to tackle, they will try somewhere that is less of a challenge. Make sure that you do not become the weak link in the home-security chain through carelessness. All it takes is one window left open or one door unlocked.

You and your parents might like to join (or even start) a neighborhood watch program. Young people can be particularly useful in this respect because they are often more informed about what is happening locally than their busy parents. Have your parents call the local police department to find out if there is one in your neighborhood and when it meets or how to start one.

REMIND YOUR PARENTS OF SOME SECURITY MEASURES

• Install good external lighting and motion-activated lights. This puts intruders in the spotlight and confuses them while giving you a good look at who is approaching.

Left: All the family should help keep the home safe. Make sure you do not become the weak link in the chain by, for example, thoughtlessly leaving a window unlatched. Burglars will exploit any unsecured lock. A study in Connecticut showed that in 41 percent of alarmed homes that were burgled, the security system was not turned on.

Dogs do not need to be ferocious to aid security. With their acute hearing, they can warn you of intruders, and their barking may frighten away criminals.

HOW LOW CAN YOU GET?

Twenty-five-year-old Sergeant Jeanette Winters was one of seven Marines killed in a plane crash on January 9, 2002, during the Afghan conflict. She was the first female U.S. Marine to die in a combat zone, and her death attracted a lot of media and public attention, including that of some local criminals. On January 27, 2002, they burgled her parents' house in Gary, Indiana, while they were at Jeanette's funeral.

- A house alarm or at least a dummy alarm prominently displayed.
- Timer switches to activate lights, radio, or television at different times. These should give the impression that someone is at home, or at least make the burglar unsure whether or not the house is empty.
- Motorized curtain cords operated by photoelectric sensors. These will close the curtains at dusk and open them again at dawn, so the would-be burglar will believe the house is occupied.
- Owning a dog or acquiring a recording of dogs barking, which can be activated when someone approaches your door.
- Secure basement and garage entry points. These are often a home's weakest points.
- All internal doors kept closed when you go out so that a potential burglar is unable to see through into all rooms and check whether there is anyone at home.
- No ladders left lying about to help burglars climb in.
- Antiburglar (nondrying) paint on drain pipes starting from six feet (1.8 m) above the ground so that pets are not harmed.
- Valuables photographed and marked, so you have a better chance of getting them back should they be stolen.
- A built-in safe.

HOME INVASION

Increased security awareness among homeowners has made life more difficult for traditional burglars. Consequently, some have joined forces and turned to home invasion. Burglars often favor daytime visits while the family is out. Home invaders, on the other hand, want to catch families at home, so they strike in the evening or on the weekends. Once they have gotten you to answer the door or gained entrance through the garage, they will descend upon you with maximum noise and threat. The idea is to terrify you into submission so that you will open the safe, tell them where the valuables are hidden, or supply keys to your car and your ATM numbers.

Adopting good habits and sticking to them is the best defense. Some home invaders seize their opportunity to attack while you are parking your car and entering the house, so be

particularly alert at these times. More often, they will just call at your door. Always use your door chain and viewers or look out a window. If you are not satisfied with unknown callers, do not let them in. Make sure your brothers and sisters know about proper procedures when someone comes to the door as well.

Installing an alarm system could make all the difference in protecting your home. Studies show that homes without security systems are about three times more likely to be broken into than homes with security systems.

Here, members of a neighborhood watch group sit around a kitchen table to put together the newsletter of the Brittany Hills, Syracuse, New York, Neighborhood Watch. The fight against crime has drawn upon America's deepest traditions of democracy and self-help.

EXTERIOR DOORS

• Should be fitted with **double mortise locks**. These are set into the wood, which makes them much stronger than locks just attached to the interior of the door.

• Hinges can be a door's weakest point, but may be strengthened with hinge bolts.

• Ordinary glass door panels can be replaced by security glazing.

• A door viewer or peephole at a height useable by most members of the family will enable the inhabitants to see who is out there before deciding whether to open the door.

• If door chains or limiters are installed, use long screws, which will withstand attempts to force an entry.

- Hollow doors are easy to smash in, but can be replaced with solid wood, fiberglass, or steel, or strengthened with steel plates or reinforcings.

WINDOWS

- Should have locks fixed with long screws to anchor them well into the wooden frame.
- Window frames should be strong and in good repair.
- If your home is particularly isolated, your parents might want to consider installing sliding metal screens on the insides of downstairs windows.

One of the best ways to protect your home is to become familiar with your neighborhood. Then you will notice whether anything is amiss or there are strangers hanging around.

DISTRACTION BURGLARIES

The elderly are particularly vulnerable to distraction burglaries, in which someone pretending to be from a local authority calls to warn them of flooding or tells them they need to check certain facilities. While one "workman" distracts the elderly person, his colleague goes to work stealing money and valuables.

• Warn elderly relatives to be careful and to risk offending people rather than let them in when they are unsure.

• The elderly should be especially cautious if they have recently had work done at the house by a casual caller. He may not come back himself, but if he realizes that there may be more money or valuables in the house, he may trade the information with a distraction burglar for a cut of the loot.

• Install door chains and viewers, and consider getting a panic alarm installed.

• Advise grandparents or other elderly relatives not to keep much money in the house, even if they think they have the perfect hiding place. Distraction burglars are well acquainted with all the likely spots.

• Keys for windows and window screens should be kept near the windows, but out of sight, and everyone in the family should know where they are. This knowledge could be vital in case of fire.

FAMILIES WILL HELP THE BURGLAR IF THEY...

• Put their names and addresses on their key rings.

• Leave a message on the answering machine that suggests that no one is at home.

• Place tempting valuables near windows, encouraging **smash and grab**.

• Forget that wedding or funeral announcements in the local press can alert a burglar to the fact that you will probably all be out or that the house of the deceased may be empty.
• Overlook the fact that burglars can go to work when you are in the house watching TV and leave again before you realize you have been robbed.

It is obvious that you are away on vacation if the curtains are left closed all day and mail or newspaper deliveries are not canceled, if a usually neat lawn is left untrimmed, or if the driveway becomes knee-deep in fallen leaves or covered with snowdrifts. Your parents could ask a neighbor or friend to deal with these possibilities while you are away. It is a good idea in any case to let neighbors know when you will be away on vacation so they can keep an eye on things while you are gone.

The Second Amendment of the Bill of Rights ensures the right of every U.S. citizen to bear arms in their own defense. Shooting intruders is a last resort, but can be a necessary action where your life, or the lives of your family, are in danger.

When an unexpected caller comes to the door, it makes sense to have a good look at them before answering. If in doubt, do not answer the door.

UNLUCKY FRIEND

Thirty-year-old Kenneth James Scott was helping his friend, Tony Young, install some stereo equipment in his home in Statesville, North Carolina. Young had gone out for a short time when suddenly, three gunmen broke down the door and demanded to know where "the box" was.

Scott insisted he did not know what they were talking about and that it was not his house. But the home invaders were not impressed. They hit him on the back of the head and threatened to kill him. Scott took them seriously and leaped out of a window to escape. As he jumped, two shots were fired, one hitting his leg. As he crawled across the front yard toward the street, the raiders fled.

IF A STRANGER COMES TO THE DOOR...

- Take a good look at the person and see if this is anyone you know or are expecting.
- Ask for identification from utility personnel and workmen. If you are unsure, call their company or workplace before letting them in.
- An after-hours caller may pretend to be delivering a package, a bouquet of flowers, or take-out food. The family might be tempted to help a deliveryman find the right house. Do not open the door, but shout through the mail slot or a window.
- Callers may claim to have had an automobile accident and wish to use the phone. Offer to call the emergency services for them.
- If your house is in a particularly isolated location or there is some desirable property on the premises, your parents might want to consider installing video surveillance cameras outside and panic buttons connected to the police inside.

Auto Theft

Stealing cars is big business. Expensive or desirable models of cars may be stolen to suit a customer's specifications and crated and shipped out of the country within hours. There is even a big trade in stolen air bags. Anything easy to steal is fine for a joyrider, although he or she prefers hot rods. They may trash them or sell them for drugs.

For committing crimes, fast cars that are not flashy or too conspicuous are the most desired. Popular models are often stolen to provide spare parts. To help combat this trade, some police auto-crime units have begun to crack down on "chop shops," where such vehicles are broken up for the spare-parts market.

Unusual models or cars in unique colors with one-time-only features are more easily identifiable. This, in turn, tends to make them less desirable to a thief. In addition, having the registration number engraved on the windows of the vehicle is a good security feature. Nobody wants the trouble or cost of having to change all the windows on a stolen car because the number scratched on the window does not match that shown on the license plates.

HOW TO PREVENT YOUR CAR FROM BEING STOLEN

Install Antitheft Devices:

If your model has poor locks, have them changed. If you are leaving your vehicle for some time, consider installing a wheel lock. To help get your car back in the event that it is stolen, install a tracking device.

Left: Car theft is big business for criminals of all kinds, including bank robbers and joyriders. There are many ways to protect your vehicle, apart from the many modern anti-theft devices. For example, try to park under a street light or any place where your car is easily visible.

Every year in the United States, more than 1.1 million vehicles are stolen. Leaving valuables visible in a car is a sure way to attract a thief. The damage he causes getting the item may cost the victim more in inconvenience than the stolen goods are worth.

Install one or more of the following:
• A steering wheel lock (usually fitted)
• An electrical kill switch
• A fuel interrupter switch
• A car alarm

Guard your keys:
• Do not leave your keys in the ignition when you get out, even for a moment.
• Do not leave your keys on a table near your door. Thieves can hook them away through the mail slot if you have one.
• Do not hide a second set of keys in your car.
• Do not attach a tag with your name and address on your car key ring.

BUMP AND ROB

A common method for stealing a car is for a robber to bump your car with another vehicle and then wait for you to get out. As you inspect the damage and attempt to exchange details, he or she grabs the opportunity to snatch your car.

If you are bumped:

• Look around to see who is in the car that has rear-ended you.

• Be particularly careful if it is a group of young males.

• If you feel uneasy, jot down the license plate number of the other car and drive to a police station or to a busy, well-lighted area, gesturing to the driver that he or she should follow you.

• If you do get out, turn off the engine and take your car keys with you, as well as your purse or wallet. Stay alert.

• Be aware that if your car has any signs on it indicating that it is a rental vehicle, you are more likely to be targeted.

• Keep your car keys separate from your house keys. Leave only an unmarked ignition key with a parking lot attendant.

• Never lend your keys (or car) to an acquaintance.

• Never give your key to a potential buyer to let him or her drive your car alone.

PARK SAFELY

Park under a streetlight, if possible. This will safeguard you and put a spotlight on a thief.

• If possible, use parking lots with an attendant on duty.

• Park with your wheels turned in toward the curb. This will make it harder for someone to push the car away, and will also mean that it will take longer for them to drive off.

• Do not leave any valuables in sight. Lock them in the trunk.
• If possible, take your stereo with you. Many stereos can be purchased with detachable faces.

MOTORCYCLES, SCOOTERS, AND BICYCLES

Two-wheeled vehicles are especially vulnerable to theft because they can be picked up and carried off or loaded onto the back of a truck. It is a good idea to use heavy chains to attach them to something stable, such as an iron railing or a block of concrete, when locking them up.

You can also install an electronic device that will immobilize the engine. Bike alarms incorporating a siren, shock sensor, and a remote panic button,

The traffic police are always on the lookout for driving offenses, whether it be speeding or spotting stolen vehicles. Traffic police carry databases listing the license plates of stolen vehicles.

This is a good example of where not to park a car. Deserted, run-down side streets are places where car thieves find it easy to steal a vehicle without being noticed or challenged. And if it is a bad neighborhood, no one is likely to try to stop them.

which will let you sound the alarm from a distance if you see your bike being tampered with, are also available. Or, you could take one of the bicycle wheels with you or detach both and put a safety bar through the wheels and frame.

CARJACKING PRECAUTIONS

Improvements in car alarms, locks, and security mechanisms have made it more difficult to steal a stationary and unoccupied vehicle. As a result, there has been a huge increase in car theft while the driver is still in the car, known as a carjacking.

Drivers distracted by young children make easier targets, and there have been some frightening instances of car thieves stealing a car and driving away with children still sitting in the back seats. The intense media interest in these crimes has caused a domino effect, encouraging copycat crimes.

Potential thieves have realized that by carjacking, they can have any car they want and the keys as well; they do not have to damage the vehicle in order to steal it. This is a huge advantage because obvious external damage can be a huge giveaway when a thief tries to sell a stolen car or is stopped by the police. The hijacking of passengers in cars is largely an opportunistic crime, so do not give thieves any opportunities. Drivers are most vulnerable to being hijacked in their cars when they:

- Have stopped at a stoplight or stop sign at an intersection.
- Have pulled into garages, parking lots, and shopping malls.
- Are using self-service gas stations and car washes.
- Are stopped at an ATM machine.
- Are stopped or slowing down at highway entrances and exits or anywhere else that drivers have to slow down or stop, such as automatic toll booths.
- Are in residential driveways or on residential streets as they get in or out of their cars.

TAIL AND SNATCH

If you are driving an expensive car in an upscale area and wearing an equally expensive watch and jewelry, be aware that you could become a victim of tail-and-snatch thieves. These thieves may not be after not your car, but rather your Rolex watch or diamond rings. An epidemic of such thefts in London has led to several deaths after victims have been followed home then jumped when they stopped outside their homes.

The increase in the crime of carjacking means motorists need to be vigilant at places where they may be open to attack, such as self-service gas stations.

How to Get In and Out of Your Car Safely

- Have your keys ready, and get into your vehicle quickly, checking around your car first to see that there is no one in the back seat.
- Lock the door behind you immediately.
- Be wary of people asking directions or handing out flyers.
- Teach brothers and sisters to get in and out of the car quickly.
- Be alert to suspicious persons sitting in other cars.
- Watch out for loitering groups of people.

On the Road

- Keep doors and windows locked and windows rolled up all the way.
- When pulling up, leave enough room ahead of you to maneuver around other cars, particularly if you sense trouble.
- Do not stop to assist anyone who is broken down. Instead, help by driving to the nearest phone, or use your cell phone to call assistance.

Worst-Case Scenario

If you are threatened with a gun, knife, or other lethal weapon, give up your vehicle without argument. Your life is more important than a car.

- Get away from the area as soon as possible. Your assailant may suddenly decide you have seen too much.
- Try to remember what the hijacker looked like.
- Report the crime immediately to police.
- If you are forced to remain in the car and drive, consider crashing into a busy intersection or at least rear-ending the vehicle ahead of you. This, of course, is a decision that depends entirely upon your own estimates of the risks involved.

CASE FILE: JUVENILE ACCUSED OF CARJACKING MURDER

In the summer of 2001, pharmacist Yvette Beakes was the victim of a carjacking near her home in Glen Burnie, Baltimore, Maryland. After driving her around town and forcing her to withdraw money from her bank accounts, the thieves took her to a nearby wooded area and there they shot her in the head.

The defense lawyer for one of the accused, 15-year-old Brian Wilson, who allegedly helped steal the car and turned up the radio to drown out the sound of the shots, thought he should be tried as a juvenile. The judge denied the petition after hearing that Wilson had been placed in a juvenile facility several times, but that his behavior became more dangerous each time he was released. This case, still being heard as we went to press,

Drivers should not get out of their cars when "bumped" on a lonely road. But if threatened with a lethal weapon, it is usually better to give up the vehicle. Some carjackers might be desperate, and it is better to do what they want than risk your life.

Giuseppe Martorana and his wife Josephine, who was shot after the couple were followed to their home, north of London, England, by thieves who stole their Rolex watches. Sadly, Josephine later died of her injuries.

re-ignited a discussion as to whether the **ban** on executing persons who were juveniles when they committed their crimes should be upheld.

CASE FILE

In August 2000, London businessman Giuseppe Martorana and his wife Josephine had been shopping at Harrods, the famous department store in London's exclusive Knightsbridge area. They were looking for a ring for Josephine to celebrate their silver wedding anniversary. Both were wearing Rolex watches.

Jason James and Darren Whyte followed the couple 20 miles (32 km) to their home at Hoddesdon, north of London, and jumped them as they unloaded their BMW. In the struggle that followed, Josephine, her son, and his girlfriend, who rushed out of the house, were all shot. As Josephine lay on the ground, Jason James straddled her and pulled off her watch. She died of her injuries three weeks later.

When the case came to court a year and a half later, the son still had a bullet in his spine and, to save her life, his girlfriend had to have her spleen and a kidney removed. Giuseppe Martorana wept in the witness box as he recalled that dreadful day. The murderous pair were found guilty and given a total of eight life sentences, the judge recommending that James should serve at least 25 years and Whyte a minimum of 20.

CALLING CARDS

As part of a crime-reduction program, Warwickshire police in England have sent cards to 40 known criminals suspected of carrying out vehicle crime in the county. The cards feature a police Range Rover and the message:

"A cut-out-and-keep reminder: If you break into people's vehicles, we'll take away your freedom—we are watching you."

Guns, Bombs, and Terrorists

How to protect yourself against firearms will, of course, depend entirely on the circumstances. But in many instances, they are the obvious ones. If someone points a gun at you, run away as fast and as far as possible, zigzagging as you go so as to present a moving target, which is much more difficult to hit. Turn a corner as soon as possible.

If the gunfire is more random, do anything to make yourself a lesser target. Stand sideways, stay as low as you can, and if possible, lie flat. Stay quiet and keep out of sight. If you can, run and hide behind something solid. Inside a building, get behind heavy objects, such as a desk, filing cabinet, or cupboard.

SCHOOL SHOOTINGS

It is not only in the United States where teachers and pupils become the target of firearm attacks. Such attacks occasionally occur in other countries as well. In fact, possibly one of the worst school shootings took place at Dunblane in Scotland, on March 13, 1996. Thomas Hamilton, a 43-year-old gun fanatic, opened fire with a variety of weapons on a classroom full of four- and five-year-olds and killed 16 of them before turning the gun on himself.

However, school shootings have occurred much more frequently in the United States and have almost always been committed by the pupils

Left: People feel at their most helpless when threatened with a gun. If you are threatened with a gun, never antagonize the gunman, who may be in an emotionally unstable state and liable to shoot.

DO NOT PLAY WITH GUNS

Never be tempted to play with guns or show them to friends without adult consent and supervision. An accident could horribly change your life as well as ending theirs.

themselves, which, so far, has not been the case elsewhere. At the time of this writing, the worst U.S. school shooting took place at Columbine High School in Littleton, Colorado, on April 20, 1999. Two pupils on a rampage killed a teacher and 12 of their fellow students and injured 23 before shooting themselves.

February 29, 2000, was just another ordinary winter's day at Buell Elementary School at Mount Morris in Michigan. Among those standing in line to go into computer class was lively, six-year-old Kayla. She had recently complained to her mother that she was being picked on by a fellow student. Suddenly that morning, this boy pulled a .32 semiautomatic handgun from his trouser pocket, pointed it at Kayla, and shot her. She died in the hospital about an hour afterward.

Later, this boy insisted he had never meant to kill Kayla, just to scare her with the gun. It turned out that the boy's father was in prison on a parole violation and his mother had been evicted from her home for nonpayment of rent two weeks earlier. So that they might continue to attend school nearby, she had sent her six- and eight-year-old sons to live with their uncle and family in what was described as "a well-known crack house."

Survivors from Columbine High School in Littleton, Colorado, hold a candle with the names of the pupils killed in the 1999 massacre. Between 1996 and 2000, 40 children lost their lives in 14 school shootings across the United States.

The place was filthy, cockroach-ridden, and littered with garbage. Under a blanket in the room of Jamelle James, a 19-year-old family friend, the boy had found the handgun. Jamelle, it was alleged, had told him where it was kept and had twirled it in front of the child.

Jamelle James was charged with involuntary manslaughter on the grounds that had he not left a loaded gun where the child could find it, the tragedy would never have occurred. He pleaded not guilty, but later changed his plea to no contest and was sentenced to 2–15 years in prison, with the order that he serve at least two years before parole.

The Columbine incident was one of a dozen U.S. school shootings during an 18-month period, and they served as a wake-up call for the nation. Things began to improve as more attention was paid to teacher training in risk assessment, prevention of bullying, conflict management, and the identification of early-warning signs.

It certainly seems a good idea to make socializing a priority, considering that so many of these lethal young men seem to be loners who find it hard to make friends, particularly with the opposite sex. Many, too, are gun and war-movie addicts and see these matters in heroic "Rambo" terms. It is possible that some input from veterans might be useful in pointing out what war is really like and how cowardly and despicable it is to shoot an unarmed person in cold blood.

BOMBS AND TERRORISTS

In Northern Ireland and mainland Britain, it has long been necessary to remain alert to the danger of bombs. Even back in Victorian times, Fenians (Irish-American activists) led bombing campaigns on London and elsewhere in Britain.

All at Once

It was certainly a night to remember. Simultaneous explosions, designed to cause the maximum public panic, were a favorite Fenian tactic. It was not

Violent, gun-toting movies that glamorize weapons and violence can encourage young people to see the use of firearms as an easy way to look big or get revenge on their enemies. Here, movie hardman Sylvester Stallone sorts out the bad guys.

The bombing of Omagh shopping center in Northern Ireland, on August 15, 1998, which killed 29 people and injured more than 300. The Real IRA, an Irish Republican splinter group, claimed responsibility for the terrorist attack.

SCHOOL RAGE TACTICS

Students should act on the assumption that prevention is the best policy by doing their best to ensure that members of their class are not left out of things or made to feel like geeks or nerds, a feeling that might make them wish to take revenge.

Be prepared. Have a look at your own school surroundings and give some thought to which might be the safest spots and quickest exits to use should the occasion arise.

the first Fenian attempt to achieve this feat, but it was the most successful.

At 9:18 P.M., on May 30, 1884, an explosion rocked a gentleman's club in Mayfair, London, injuring 12 of the domestic staff. Fifteen seconds later, there was another explosion, this time at the nearby home of Member of Parliament, Sir Watkin Williams Wynn. One lady in the party gathered in the drawing room suffered a minor cut to her hand. Two servants were also injured, one of them "somewhat severely."

Less than two minutes later, another bomb wrecked the offices of Scotland Yard's Criminal Investigation Department and Special Irish Branch. Fortunately, the last of the detectives had just gone home, but a uniformed constable nearby and two cab drivers were injured by flying debris. At the same time, a boy spotted a black bag lying close to one of the lion statues at the foot of Nelson's Column in Trafalgar Square. On examination, this was found to contain an "infernal machine" primed with eight pounds (3.6 kg) of American-brand dynamite, a substance not licensed for import to Britain.

Ireland achieved virtual independence within the British Commonwealth with the Anglo-Irish Treaty of 1921, but the six northeastern counties (which were largely Protestant) opted for self-government within the United Kingdom. However, the Irish Republican

Army (IRA) continued to resist partition. Another mainland Britain bombing campaign was mounted in 1939, and hostilities were again resumed in 1972, when the IRA left a bomb at Aldershot army barracks. This one killed five women cleaners, a gardener, and a priest.

"The Troubles" Again

Many bombing and shooting incidents followed, on railroad stations, trains, clubs, pubs, through the mail, and at outdoor events. Some bombs contained "Belfast confetti," which was a mixture of nuts, bolts, and nails designed to kill and maim as many people as possible. If you visit London and wonder why there are so few garbage cans at train stations, it is because they were a favorite bomb-dumping ground for the IRA.

Of course, Northern Ireland itself suffered much, much more. The IRA and the Ulster Defence Regiment fought it out, resulting in the deaths of thousands of citizens. It is hoped that the bombing in a busy Omagh shopping center on August 15, 1998, which killed 29 people and injured 300, was the final Irish tragedy.

The threat of terrorism is now also very much on the minds of U.S. citizens, but the threat of bombs is not new here either. Early in the 20th century, bombs were planted for political reasons (by anarchists and at fiercely fought election meetings in Irish and Italian neighborhoods) and by the Mafia as a means of persuasion.

BOMBINGS IN THE U.S.

During the 1980s and 1990s, the U.S. fell prey to the lethal attentions of the Unabomber and Puerto Rican nationalists. From 1974 to 1983, the Puerto Rican nationalist group FALN staged no fewer than 120 bombings and **incendiary** attacks in the United States. One of these, in a historic New York tavern, resulted in four deaths and caused injuries to 68 people. Other incidents blinded a policeman in one eye (ironically, he was a Puerto Rican) and blew the foot off another.

FIGHTING TERRORISM

The key to helping combat terrorism is to keep alert and aware of your surroundings so that you notice anything unusual. Do not ignore unattended luggage or packages left at airports, railroad stations, and bus stations in places where they might not seem out of place.

Many of the IRA's bombs in London were left in suitcases at railroad or subway stations. Inform someone in authority if you see anything suspicious. And do not leave any of your own packages and cases unattended: you could cause unnecessary havoc. Never open suspicious packages or letters, and always report suspicious behavior.

The perpetrators were finally caught with thousands of rounds of ammunition and 24 pounds (11 kg) of unstable dynamite under their floorboards, and plans to assist a prison break and blow up the National Armory. The prosecution was long-delayed while the constitutionality of the FBI having gathered evidence using closed-circuit television in the suspect's meeting place was argued, right up to the Supreme Court.

"Finally," says Candice DeLong in her book, *Special Agent*, "the justices ruled in the Bureau's favor, affirming that the privacy guaranteed by the Bill of Rights did not extend to making bombs at home." The leaders eventually stood trial in 1985, and were convicted of **seditious** conspiracy and other charges. Their supporters claim that FALN aims were just like those of Nelson Mandela in his fight for black freedom in South Africa or even George Washington's against the British. President Clinton released them in 1999.

When Professor Linda Kaczynski was reading the *Washington Post* one day in the autumn of 1995, she noticed something disturbingly familiar about the **manifesto** published there. The attitude, opinions, and even turns of phrase reminded her

Theodore John Kaczynski, "the Unabomber," was arrested in April 1996. Between 1978 and 1995, he killed and maimed several people with explosives, some of which were sent through the U.S. mail.

of letters from Ted, her brother-in-law, whom she had never met, but whom she knew was odd.

She was horrified, not so much of the ideas therein—that science and technology were a disaster—but because the manifesto purported to come from the Unabomber, a man whose activities had been maiming and killing people over the past 15 years.

During that time, the FBI had tried desperately to find him, but the United States is a big place. Endless hours were spent attempting to trace his typewriter and, since airlines and universities were the main targets, examining thousands of airline and university records. Even a group of student "Dungeons and Dragons" players were looked at seriously. However, all these efforts proved fruitless.

David Kaczynsky was not convinced that the manifesto was his brother's work until he found an old essay of Ted's that was too similar in content to leave any doubts, and approaches were made to the authorities.

Surveillance was placed on Ted Kaczynsky, who lived in isolation in a tumbledown hut in Montana. Eventually, by April 1996, sufficient evidence had been gathered for a raid on his hut, which was found to contain more bombs in the making.

The Unabomber had written to one of his badly injured victims, Yale computer scientist David Gelernter, saying that obviously, people with advanced degrees were not as smart as they thought they were. "If you'd had any brains, you would have realized that there are a lot of people out there who resent bitterly the way you techno-nerds are changing the world and you wouldn't have been dumb enough to open an unexpected package from an unknown source."

That is good advice. Do not open unexpected packages. But Ted, an academic himself, was being a vile **hypocrite** here. On Gerlenter's package, he had put the return address of another academic who would have been known to the scientist. He is now serving life imprisonment without the possibility of parole.

Fraud, Forgery, and Confidence Tricks

Frauds, con tricks, or scams come in many and varied forms. Most con artists tempt their victims with get-rich-quick schemes or by offering them goods more cheaply than usual or even for free.

Some con tricks are complex, while others are merely minor diversionary tactics used while you are relieved of something more precious. For example, one trick is for a person to drop a 10-dollar bill and pretend it is yours just as you are about to take your card out of the cash machine. In the split second it takes you to pick the money up, they can snatch your card and be off.

There is a simple rule of thumb for dealing with any something-for-nothing, get-rich-quick scheme and it is easy to remember. If it seems too good to be true, then it probably is.

BOGUS PRIZES

A common modern sales scheme, which is really a bit of a con trick, is the bogus prize. Always beware of exciting phone callers who tell you that you have won an exotic vacation when you do not recall having entered any such contest. The prize is usually merely a selling ploy, and the extras you have to pay out to claim it can amount to a substantial sum. Again, if it seems too good to be true, it probably is.

Left: It is easy to fall for phone and Internet con tricks, such as bogus prizes or promised free vacation packages. Protect yourself by becoming aware of the latest scams and never give personal details to unknown callers.

CONFIDENCE-TRICK LETTERS

If you are the owner of a business, you may become prey to another modern scam: the confidence-trick letter. In recent years, there has been a surge in confidence-trick letters, both by regular mail and e-mail. These may ask if they may pass some money through your bank account, while giving you a good commission. They claim that some silly local rule bars them from doing it through their own account. In the process they will, of course, need access to your bank details.

Anyone can be a potential target. The perpetrators are not always so smart. Sir Paul Condon even received one while he was commissioner of the Metropolitan Police in London, England.

Some con artists specialize in placing large orders with businesses in prosperous countries other than their own, which makes them difficult to trace. Sometimes they target small companies, who will naturally be delighted with this unexpected windfall. The letterheads are impressive and

HISTORIC FORGERS

Two of the most successful Victorian counterfeiters were Americans Macdonnel and Noyes Bidwell, who, after leaving the U.S. in 1874, cut a fraudulent path across Europe and South America. They ended up in Britain, where they defrauded the Bank of England of upward of £100,000 sterling, then a much larger amount than it is even now. But they made a mistake, missing a date off a note, and were sent to prison for life.

During the 1870s, London was also home to many Russian refugees. They set up businesses forging Russian rubles (the Russian currency) and swamped their old country with them. Poor farmers and peasants bore the brunt of the losses, and the economic stability of the country was threatened.

Anyone can be the target of confidence-trick letters. One was even sent to Sir Paul Condon when he was commissioner of the London Metropolitan Police in England.

genuine-looking but, if you succumb, kiss your goods goodbye and do not expect any payment. The impressive firm will have disappeared back into the woodwork.

A great number of these con letters come out of West Africa. In Britain, the police refer to them as "419s" because that is the number of the penal code in one of the offending countries that makes sending them an offense. Most losses amount to a few thousand dollars, but the biggest loss yet recorded is about U.S. $41 million from a wealthy mother and daughter who received a 419 from Hong Kong.

Due to its global nature, the crime is particularly difficult to investigate. You should examine such letters carefully and pass them on to the police.

COUNTERFEIT MONEY

If you find a forged note or a counterfeit coin among your money, you will feel you have been cheated. However, their circulation can have a far more serious effect on the financial stability of your country. For this reason, knowingly forging or passing forged currency has always been severely punished. At one time, forgers were often sentenced to death, but later, a life sentence or a long term of imprisonment with hard labor became the rule.

Counterfeiting has long been a problem. In 1865, the U.S. Secret Service was created to curtail the crime. Banks have had to work hard to keep one step ahead of the forgers by using special paper and inks and developing more complex designs.

The U.S. dollar is the most counterfeited currency in the world because it is universally accepted and trusted. To tell whether a banknote is genuine, check it against genuine notes. There are several tell-tale signs.

CHECKING YOUR CHANGE

To determine whether or not your money is counterfeit or real, consider the following.

Banknotes:

- Genuine currency paper has tiny red and blue fibers embedded throughout. Counterfeiters often try to simulate these by printing them on top of the paper.
- Use a detector pen or compare it with a banknote of similar denomination to see if the paper is the same thickness and quality. Check also that the embossing feels the same. (Some forged banknotes feel flat.)
- Check that all the tiny details of the **hatching** and patterns are identical.
- On counterfeit notes, lines are often blurred around the edges.
- The counterfeit portrait may be lifeless and dull in comparison with the genuine article.
- Check the colors.

Coins:

- Examine the coin. Feel the weight. This may differ from that of the genuine article.
- Take a close look at the details on the coin. The **milling** or words around the edges may be ragged or imprecise and the definition on the face less accurate. The president's head may be of a different size.

If you discover a counterfeit banknote or coin, if possible, record how and when you got it. Handle it as little as possible to preserve any fingerprints. Place it in an envelope to protect it and take it to the police.

CYBER CRIME

Far from being the information superhighway that some call it, the Internet has been likened to a muddy road in the 17th century, with robbers and

An Italian financial policeman compares a genuine Euro coin (left) with a counterfeit discovered in Naples, southern Italy. The counterfeit coin is made of only one metal, while the real one contains two elements.

highwaymen lurking around every bend, ready to attack. Or, as Washington High School students working on a special Internet project for the State Attorney General's Office put it; "The Internet is crawling with scamming scum."

But what can you do to protect yourself when using the World Wide Web? Knowledge is your best defense from those that would harm you and steal your money. Along with that, you can use the assistance of a few defensive measures; for example, always stay informed of the latest and most common scams and the defense tactics to use against them. For a start, use one of the less-vulnerable software programs and install a good virus-protection program.

MORE SELF-DEFENSE TACTICS

- Never reveal your password to anyone. Once a hacker has your password, he can cost you a fortune by charging all his bills to you.

- Never reveal personal details to anyone who asks for them for no good reason. Even if you receive official-sounding e-mails requesting these details from someone claiming to be from your Internet Service Provider or someone in authority, like the police, do not do it. Never give this information without checking with your parents or someone else in authority first.

Modern-day highwaymen are waiting out on the Internet in the hope of waylaying the unwary Web traveler. Credit cards should be used with care over the Internet. Look for the locked padlock symbol in the browser window that indicates a secure site, and deal only with well-known and reputable companies.

DEFENDING YOURSELF AGAINST HACKERS

Your password should be easy for you to remember, but difficult for other people to guess. Do not use the names of family members or a pet, addresses, phone numbers, dates of birth, or the maiden name of your mother or anyone else. Do not connect it in any way with your hobbies or pastimes—for example, using the password "Home Run" if you play baseball or "Quarterback" if you are a football fan. Do not use any word that appears in a dictionary. If the hacker knows you personally, he or she will try all these ideas. Even if he does not know you, he can run through the many possibilities, or try and find your personal information elsewhere. There is even software available for cracking passwords. Never fool yourself into thinking that a hacker would not bother to get to you. Some hackers are relentless and can be vicious.

You can protect yourself by making your password long. Always choose an unlikely combination of letters and digits, such as, 15CABBAGE27GEORGE. Check the service provider's recommendations —usually there is a link on the page where you select your password.

You can check the latest scams by logging on to one of the Web pages that keep an eye on such things. There is ZDNet's E-Hoax Central or Dr. Solomon's Hoax Page. This information changes constantly.

E-Mail Security

Just as you can keep your computer safe, there are things you can do to keep your e-mail safe as well.

Viruses

Computer viruses are programs designed to spread themselves by first infecting another program or the operating system and then making copies of themselves, which are passed on to other computers without the knowledge of the computer user.

The effects of viruses vary. Some are designed to damage files or interfere

WAR BANKNOTES

Forgery has been deliberately used as an instrument of war. When the Duke of Wellington was about to enter France to fight Napoleon in 1815, he asked for forgers in his armies to come forward to turn English sovereigns into "napoleons." He wanted these so he could buy supplies from French peasants. The coins were made of gold, however, so they would retain their value. Napoleon himself had produced rubles for his invasion of Russia in 1812, and Hitler had pound sterling banknotes manufactured with which to flood Britain to destabilize the country during World War II.

Today, the U.S. dollar is the most counterfeited currency because it is almost universally accepted and trusted. Large amounts have been manufactured in North Korea, Russia, and Colombia, and there have been claims of a joint Iranian-Syrian conspiracy to weaken the U.S. by producing counterfeit dollars.

System Scan Status   **?**

System Scan

Last file scanned

C:\Program Files\Network Associates\VirusScan\Confwiz.exe

Statistics

Scanned:	4673	Deleted:	0
Infected:	0	Moved:	0
Cleaned:	0		

Disable   Properties   Close

Viruses can make your computer sick, and possibly destroy it altogether. It is worth paying for a good virus-protection program and also learning about the latest scams and viruses from hoax-busting Web sites.

with the working of your computer. Others are less malicious and want only to spread themselves around, but even these are harmful, as they damage files and can cause other problems. Most are spread through attachments in e-mail messages. In most cases, the virus can be freed only if the attachment is opened.

Most people pick up computer viruses through ignorance or carelessness. However, they can be avoided:

• Beware of out-of-character subject lines, such as "I Love You," supposedly from your math teacher.

• Always scan floppy disks using antivirus software if they have been used in another computer—even disks from your best friends.

• Do not open attachments ending in .exe, .vbs, .com, or .dll even if you know, or think you know, the sender. Viruses can appear to come from friends. If in doubt, phone the friend or check with one of the hoax-busting sites.

PROTECTING CHILDREN

Children should be warned never to give any personal details over the Internet, even if the person in the chat room seems respectable. Remind them it is easy to fake an identity on the Internet and that even if the contact does prove to be an apparently trustworthy person, such as a doctor, teacher, clergyman, policeman, or lawyer, they can still prove to be a danger to children. They must also be warned never, ever to arrange to meet anyone whom they have met in a chat room without first obtaining a guardian's permission.

CASE HISTORY: FRAUD IN THE 1920s

Con artists gather where the best pickings seem to be. These days, it is on the Internet, but in 1920, it was fashionable European cities and resorts. The wealthy, who had been denied their pleasures during World War I, flocked back. With them, came a horde of con artists. There were so many in London that Scotland Yard was obliged to form a special anti-con squad, headed by a Detective Inspector Leech, to combat them.

Most of the con artists were Americans or Australians. They mixed with the wealthy and looked and sounded just like them: well traveled,

FIGHTING CYBER CRIME

Given the global nature of cyber crime, it is difficult to police. However, efforts are being made. For example, the American government set up the U.S. Internet Fraud Complaints Center in 2001. It soon gathered information from 56,000 victims of scams ranging from online auctions to pyramid schemes. It brought 90 prosecutions as a result. This is a drop in the ocean, but it is a start. U.S. Attorney General John Ashcroft referred to the new organization as "a cyber-community watch program."

charming, and elegant, but never loud.

One of Detective Inspector Leech's team, Detective Inspector Percy J. Smith, met so many, he wrote a book entitled simply, *Con Men*. He recalled an incident in which they had tried to warn a "mark," a wealthy American, that his new friend—acquired on a ship as they crossed the Atlantic—was Davidson, a known con man.

Their advice was far from welcome. The recipient resented the intrusion into his private affairs and insisted that he had not entered into any business deals with Davidson nor drawn out any large sums of money lately. However, neither statement was true, and as he spoke, £5,000 sterling in

Teenagers playing computer games in a Hong Kong Internet café. The Hong Kong government has proposed a series of measures to raise safety standards and prevent the cafés from becoming crime hotspots.

banknotes were sitting in his pocket. It was, he said, for an investment in a "sure thing."

The detectives did not realize that the American's "quiet friend," who had been sitting with them while the warning was taking place, was also one of the con men. He acted with the resource typical of the breed, jumping to his feet, saying he thought the detectives were impostors, probably a gang trying to relieve them of their cash. He was going to make sure that his was in a place of safety.

The pair hurriedly took a cab to Selfridge's Department Store, where the quiet friend told the American to hold the cab while he deposited his cash in his safety deposit box. The now-frightened man exclaimed, "Here, put mine in as well." The quiet friend went in the front door of Selfridge's and straight out the back. It was "a sad and chastened man" who later related the story to DI Smith.

CASE HISTORY: FRAUD TODAY

Some scams rely on our natural concern for our own health or safety and can most easily be perpetrated by those in whom we naturally put our trust, such as lawyers or doctors. In February 2002, Dr. Felix Vasquez-Ruiz, a Chicago doctor, was convicted of fraud. He had performed thousands of medically unnecessary tests that had involved painful shocks to patients' arms and legs.

The prosecution alleged that over a period of 15 years, he had benefited to the tune of around $2.5 million from health care funds. He had selected factory workers who had medical insurance and told them they needed these expensive nerve-conduction tests. Meanwhile, he falsified their medical records to say that the patients had complained of searing pains in their arms, legs, and backs. Twenty-nine patients testified that they had never had the pains he described. The prosecution also claimed that, in addition, he had ordered unnecessary expensive ultrasound and allergy tests. Dr. Vasquex-Ruiz was convicted on 27 counts of fraud.

GLOSSARY

Ban: to prohibit

Communication alarm: alarms found on public transport for the purpose of warning the driver or stopping the vehicle

Counterfeit (v.): to make fraudulent copies of something

Double mortise lock: a door lock where the key is turned twice, to secure a door or entrance for extra safety

Epidemic: excessively prevalent

Estranged: implies the development of indifference or hostility with consequent separation or divorce

Hatching: a series of finely drawn lines, usually close together

Hypocrite: a person who puts on a false appearance of virtue

Incendiary: a bomb

Manifesto: a written statement declaring publicly the intentions, motives, or views of its issuer

Milling: a corrugated edge on a coin

Personal alarm: a small electronic device that a person can carry with them and activate if they feel threatened

Pickpocket: a thief who steals by taking things from people's clothing or personal baggage

Predator: someone who preys on others, often planning to steal from them or assault them in some way; predators most often continue to choose the same type of victim, such as young women or boys

Pyramid scheme: an investment swindle in which some early investors are paid off with money put up by later ones in order to encourage more and bigger risks

Ruse: a subterfuge in order to distract someone's attention

Seditious: of, relating to, or tending toward an incitement of resistance to or insurrection against lawful authority

Smash and grab: a term used to describe a method of stealing, where thieves break windows (for example, on a shopfront or a car) to grab the goods within before fleeing

Spiked (v): to add a drug, such as sleeping pills, to a drink without the drinker realizing

Stalker: someone who has an obsessive interest in another person, which leads him or her to follow this person, make telephone calls, and pester him or her in other ways; some stalkers attack and sometimes kill their victims

Tap (v.): to cut in on a telephone conversation as a means of getting information

CHRONOLOGY

1812: Napoleon counterfeits rubles before invading Russia.

1815: Wellington counterfeits napoleons before Waterloo.

1870: Russian rubles counterfeited in London.

1884: Simultaneous Fenian explosions in London.

1920: Con artists are at work in London.

1921: Anglo-Irish Agreement.

1939: IRA explosions in London.

1967: First murder by Fred West.

1972: IRA bombing campaign in London.

1974: FALN bombs in the United States; Bundy murders begin.

1978: Bundy murders end; Gallego murders Kippi Vaught; Unabomber starts his campaign.

1983: End of FALN campaign in the United States.

1990: California passes anti-stalking law.

1993: Bomb explodes at World Trade Center, New York; stalking of Robert Fine begins.

1994: Fred West arrested for multiple murders.

1995: Rose West convicted of murder; Unabomber's manifesto published; end of stalking of Robert Fine.

1996: Massacre of young children at Dunblane School, Scotland; Unabomber arrested.

1997: Oldest British stalker convicted; U.K. anti-stalking law passed; Sheila Bellush murdered.

1998: Unabomber sentenced to life in prison.

1999: Release of FALN terrorists; massacre at Columbine School, Littleton, Colorado.

2000: Sheila Bellush's murderers convicted; six-year-old kills fellow pupil in Michigan; Josephine Martorana shot by Rolex thieves.

2001:   Terrorist attack on World Trade Center; U.S. Internet Frauds Complaints Center established; five overseas students mugged in Troy; Columbia University administrator mugged.

2002:   Chicago doctor convicted of fraud; killers of Josephine Martorana sentenced to life; Warwickshire police send "greeting cards" to car thieves; Marine sergeant's parents house burgled while out attending her funeral.

FURTHER INFORMATION

Useful Web Sites

www.crimedoctor.com/homeinvasion.htm

www.weprevent.org/USA/cover.pdf

www.antistalking.com/iknowyou.htm

www.soshelp.org

www.aware.org/

www.kumite.com/myths

www.drsolomon.com

www.cyberangels.com

www.hoaxkill.com

www.tinman.org/edge/062100.html

Further Reading

Aftab, Parry. *A Parents' Guide to the Internet and How to Protect Your Children in Cyberspace*. New York: McGraw-Hill, 2000.

Becker, Gavin De. *Protecting the Gift: Keeping Children and Teenagers Safe (And Parents Sane)*. New York: DTP, 2000.

Becker, Gavin De. *Fear Less: Real Truth about Risk, Safety, and Security in a Time of Terrorism*. New York: Little Brown, 2002.

Davis, Dr. Joseph A. (editor). *Stalking Crimes and Victim Protection*. Boca Raton: CRC Press, 2001.

Gallagher, Richard. *I'll Be Watching You*. London: Virgin, 2002.

Gross, Linda. *Surviving a Stalker: Everything You Need to Know to Keep Yourself Safe*. New York: Marlow & Co., 2000.

Perkins, John, Al Ridenhour, and Matt Kovsky. *Attack Proof: The Ultimate Guide to Personal Protection.* New York: Human Kinetics, 2000.

Piven, Joshua and David Borgenich. *The Worst-Case Scenario Handbook.* San Francisco: Chronicle Books, 1999.

Scott, Yolanda M. *Fear of Crime among Inner-City African Americans.* New York: LFB Scholarly Publishing, 2001.

Wright, Cynthia. *Everything You Need to Know about Dealing with Stalking.* New York: Rosen Publishing Group, 1999.

About the Author

A former officer with the Metropolitan Police in London, England, Joan Lock is an experienced writer specializing in police and criminal matters. Her non-fiction crime titles include *Lady Policeman, The British Policewoman, Marlborough Street: The Story of a London Court, Dreadful Deeds and Awful Murders, Scotland Yard Casebook,* and *Tales from Bow Street.*

Joan is also the author of four crime novels and was a regular contributor to *Police Review* magazine. She has also written dramatic plays and feature programs for BBC radio in England.

INDEX